ORIENTEERING

D1738037

BOY SCOUTS OF AMERICA

Requirements

1. Show that you know first aid for the types of injuries that could occur while orienteering, including cuts, scratches, blisters, snakebite, insect stings, tick bites, heat and cold reactions (sunburn, heatstroke, heat exhaustion, hypothermia), and dehydration. Explain to your counselor why you should be able to identify poisonous plants and poisonous animals that are found in your area.

2. Explain what orienteering is.

3. Do the following:

   a. Explain how a compass works. Describe the features of an orienteering compass.

   b. In the field, show how to take a compass bearing and follow it.

4. Do the following:

   a. Explain how a topographic map shows terrain features. Point out and name five terrain features on a map and in the field.

   b. Point out and name 10 symbols on a topographic map.

   c. Explain the meaning of *declination.* Tell why you must consider declination when using map and compass together.

   d. Show a topographic map with magnetic north-south lines.

   e. Show how to measure distances on a map using an orienteering compass.

   f. Show how to orient a map using a compass.

35925
ISBN 978-0-8395-3385-6
©2003 Boy Scouts of America
2010 Printing

BANG/Brainerd, MN
12-2010/061063

5. Set up a 100-meter pace course. Determine your walking and running pace for 100 meters. Tell why it is important to pace-count.

6. Do the following:

   a. Identify 20 international control description symbols. Tell the meaning of each symbol.

   b. Show a control description sheet and explain the information provided.

   c. Explain the following terms and tell when you would use them: attack point, collecting feature, aiming off, contouring, reading ahead, handrail, relocation, rough versus fine orienteering.

7. Do the following:

   a. Take part in three orienteering events. One of these must be a cross-country course.

   b. After each event, write a report with (1) a copy of the master map and control description sheet, (2) a copy of the route you took on the course, (3) a discussion of how you could improve your time between control points, and (4) a list of your major weaknesses on this course. Describe what you could do to improve.

8. Do ONE of the following:

   a. Set up a cross-country course that is at least 2,000 meters long with at least five control markers. Prepare the master map and control description sheet.

   b. Set up a score orienteering course with at least 12 control points and a time limit of at least 60 minutes. Set point values for each control. Prepare the master map and control description sheet.

9. Act as an official during an orienteering event. This may be during the running of the course you set up for requirement 8.

10. Teach orienteering techniques to your patrol, troop, or crew.

Contents

Note to the Counselor

While orienteering is primarily an individual sport, BSA Youth Protection procedures call for using the buddy system. Requirement 7a can be completed by pairs or groups of Scouts.

What Is Orienteering?

Since ancient times, rough maps of the Earth and simple compasses have guided explorers, warriors, and pioneers like Lewis and Clark, Marco Polo, Christopher Columbus, and Amelia Earhart. Often, their skills with map and compass were all that kept these men and women from disaster.

What has been a vital skill for humans for thousands of years is now a sport—orienteering. In 1919, a Swedish Scout leader, Major Ernst Killander, decided that compasses and maps could be used for fun as well as survival and navigation. Sport orienteering was born on that day, as 155 contestants fanned out around Stockholm with compasses and maps.

The sport's popularity has grown steadily. The International Orienteering Federation was formed in 1961, and Orienteering USA followed in 1971. Orienteering is now a recognized sport at the Olympic Games, and thousands of people participate in the sport each year in local clubs and competitions. There are more than 60 clubs in the United States alone. The Boy Scouts of America has long included orienteering in its program, from local patrol events to national Boy Scout orienteering contests drawing more than ,000 participants. The Orienteering merit badge is your invitation to explore this exciting activity.

By definition, *orienteering* is a cross-country race in which participants use a highly detailed map and a compass to navigate their way between checkpoints along an unfamiliar course.

Using a Compass

Earth is a giant magnet with two ends, a north magnetic pole and a south magnetic pole. The poles are areas where the lines of magnetic force come together and are strongest. Even at distances of thousands of miles, the poles exert a pull on magnetized minerals. The Chinese were probably the first to discover this between 4,000 and 5,000 years ago when they noticed that lodestone or magnetite, if allowed to swing freely, would always point in a north-south direction. By carving a small pointer of this mineral and then floating it on a liquid, they invented the first compass. Once they added a *compass card,* showing the major directions, they could follow those directions relative to the Earth's magnetic field.

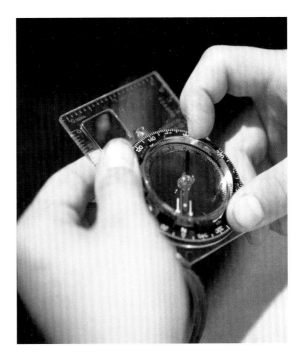

Today's compass has not changed much from those early models. Basic compasses combine a compass card showing 16 or 32 points of the compass or 360 degrees of a circle, and a magnetized metal needle that is colored on the north end.

The thumb compass rides on the thumb and simplifies map orientation and direction finding while you are on the move. It suffers a bit in accuracy, however, especially in the hands of a novice.

The *compass rose* has appeared on maps since the 14th century. A Portuguese mapmaker drew the first 32-point compass rose with a fleur-de-lis— familiar to all Scouts— indicating north and a cross indicating east toward the Holy Land.

Types of Orienteering Compasses

Orienteering compasses fall into two categories: *thumb compasses* and *baseplate* or *protractor compasses.*

Special Features of Orienteering Compasses

The *bearing index* and *direction-of-travel arrow* are located on the baseplate. Degrees on a rotating 360-degree bezel are read against the *index line.* The direction-of-travel arrow, found at the far end of the index line, indicates which way to go after you have taken a bearing.

Map scales, such as the 1:15,000 scale commonly found on orienteering maps or the 1:24,000 and 1:62,500 scales found on U.S. Geological Survey topographic maps, may be marked along the edges of the compass's baseplate. *Inch and millimeter scales* may appear as well. These scales simplify measuring distance on a map.

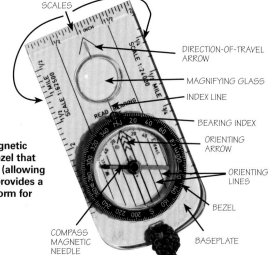

SCALES

DIRECTION-OF-TRAVEL ARROW

MAGNIFYING GLASS

INDEX LINE

BEARING INDEX

ORIENTING ARROW

ORIENTING LINES

BEZEL

BASEPLATE

COMPASS MAGNETIC NEEDLE

The baseplate compass, a magnetic needle within a 360-degree bezel that rotates on a clear plastic base (allowing maps to be read beneath it), provides a convenient and accurate platform for working with bearings.

An *orienting arrow* is embossed on the transparent base of the circular compass housing. You use the orienting arrow by aligning it with the needle so that you can take a bearing or establish your direction of travel when a bearing is known. When used along with a map, it allows you to orient the map and take a bearing from the map.

North-south or *orienting lines* lie parallel to the orienting arrow on the base of the compass housing. You use these lines when taking a bearing from a map and when identifying landmarks using a compass and a map.

The *magnetic needle* of an orienteering compass is fast setting so that the orienteer wastes no time waiting for the needle to come to rest.

Taking a Bearing

Taking a bearing is simply measuring a direction from one point on the ground to another. Hold the compass in one hand, centered on your body. Rotate your body and the compass until the direction-of-travel arrow points in the direction you want to go. Rotate the bezel of the compass until the north end of the magnetic arrow (usually red) lines up with the north end of the orienting arrow. Determine the bearing by reading the number on the bezel directly opposite the bearing index.

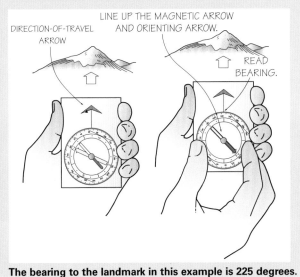

The bearing to the landmark in this example is 225 degrees.

Using a Topographic Map

A map is a two-dimensional representation of a three-dimensional space. It strives to reproduce on a sheet of paper, by using symbols, all the features of a piece of land or water.

If you walk all the way around the base of a mountain and always stay at the exact same elevation, you are contouring around it. The line you follow is called a *contour line*. Now do it again, only walk a line 20 feet higher in elevation. You have walked a second contour line. The *contour interval* between the two lines is 20 feet.

The contour interval varies from map to map. The contour interval for most USGS maps is 20 or 40 feet, while for most orienteering maps it is 3 or 5 meters. The amount of the interval is usually shown on the map. Find the contour interval on the lower right-hand corner of the full-color centerfold map of Sid Richardson Scout Ranch in this pamphlet.

You also can figure out the contour interval. Here's how. Determine the number of contour lines between the two adjacent index contours; add 1 to this figure, then divide by the elevation difference. Usually, an *index contour* occurs every fifth line. It is a bolder brown than the other contour lines, and on most

A *topographic map* tries to show the form of the land including relief, or elevation, by the use of contour lines.

To understand how relief can be represented by a flat map, imagine a hilly island in the middle of a lake. The shoreline is its lowest contour line. If the water rises 20 feet in the lake, the shoreline will be higher up the hill. If you were to draw these two lines on a sheet of paper, the upper line would lie inside the lower one. Each rise in water level will result in a line that you could draw inside the preceding one. These rings represent a topographic or contour map of the hill.

GENTLE SLOPE

STEEP SLOPE

CLIFFS

MOUNTAIN SUMMIT

VALLEY OR GULLY

RIDGE

maps you will find a number on it that tells its elevation above sea level. On orienteering maps, the index contour line does not have an elevation number, but is thicker than the others and is used as a guide for the eye.

You can also "see" the shape of the terrain from the profile of the lines on the paper. If a mountain is perfectly conical like a wizard's hat, the contour lines depicting the mountain will look like a bull's-eye. Each contour line will be perfectly circular, and all will be the same distance apart. More likely, however, the mountain is irregular. At one part of the mountain, the contour line may intersect a valley or a depression. If the contour line ran into the valley, it would lose elevation and would no longer be considered the same contour line. In order to continue indicating the same elevation on the mountain, the line goes up slightly and then drops back down at the other side of the valley, creating an upward-pointing V shape. When a higher point like a ridge is encountered, the contour line will "V" downward.

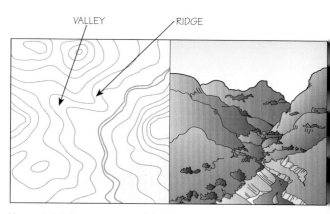

Upward "V's" on a topographical map are valleys, and downward "V's" represent ridges.

The illustrations here show some important elements. If two contour lines are far apart, it would take a long horizontal distance to climb that distance on the map—the land is relatively flat at that point or just a gentle slope. If they are close together (steep), or almost touching (a cliff), getting up the next few feet will be hard!

Map Features

Most maps include a scale relating distance on the map to distances on the actual terrain, and symbols representing features on the ground. The scale is represented as a ratio. Common scales on orienteering maps are 1:5,000, 1:7,500, 1:10,000, and 1:15,000, while scales of 1:24,000, 1:62,500, and 1:250,000 are used for other types of maps. The fraction means that one unit of measurement on the map is equal to a certain number of like units on the actual terrain. So on a map with a scale of 1:24,000, 1 inch on the map equals 24,000 inches on the ground, or 2,000 feet. On a map with a 1:62,500 scale, 1 inch equals 62,500 inches, or approximately 1 mile.

> The smaller the second number in the ratio, the smaller the area covered, and the more detail the map will show.

Accompanying the fractional scale of the map are distance rulers—visual representations of the map's scale. Three rulers are common: one in miles, one in thousands of feet, and for orienteering maps, one in meters and kilometers. These are used to convert a distance between two places on the map to a distance between the same two places on the ground.

Find the scale and the distance ruler on the Sid Richardson Scout Ranch map in this pamphlet.

Maps are artistic representations of reality. All land features on maps are represented by symbols, which may represent the same features from map to map. But symbols can vary, depending on the mapmaker's preference, the map's intended purpose, and the country of origin. Therefore, a map usually will have a legend to help identify the symbols. For example, the legend of the Sid Richardson Scout Ranch map shows symbols defined for terrain features such as earthbanks, cliffs, boulders, lakes, power lines, and buildings.

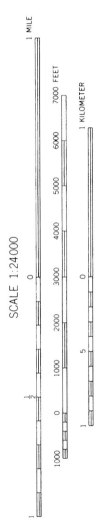

Colors on Maps

Color is used to further define map symbols. Orienteering maps are five-color maps, using black, brown, blue, green, and yellow printed on white. The descriptions below apply only to orienteering maps. Refer to the legends of other maps for identification of symbols and colors.

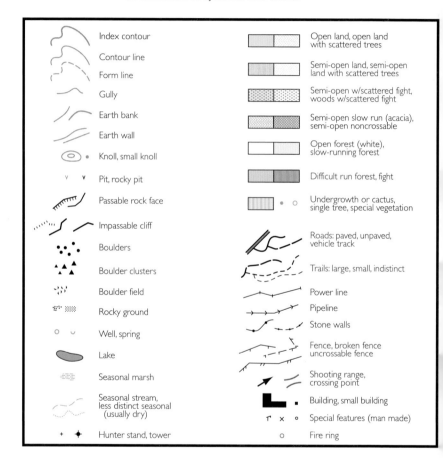

Index contour	Open land, open land with scattered trees
Contour line	Semi-open land, semi-open land with scattered trees
Form line	Semi-open w/scattered fight, woods w/scattered fight
Gully	Semi-open slow run (acacia), semi-open noncrossable
Earth bank	Open forest (white), slow-running forest
Earth wall	Difficult run forest, fight
Knoll, small knoll	Undergrowth or cactus, single tree, special vegetation
Pit, rocky pit	Roads: paved, unpaved, vehicle track
Passable rock face	Trails: large, small, indistinct
Impassable cliff	Power line
Boulders	Pipeline
Boulder clusters	Stone walls
Boulder field	Fence, broken fence uncrossable fence
Rocky ground	Shooting range, crossing point
Well, spring	Building, small building
Lake	Special features (man made)
Seasonal marsh	Fire ring
Seasonal stream, less distinct seasonal (usually dry)	
Hunter stand, tower	

Black: Anything constructed by people, including roads, trails, houses, buildings, railroads, power lines, dams, bridges, and boundaries. Paved roads and improved gravel roads are solid black lines. Unimproved roads (jeep trails) are represented by broken black lines. Trails are thinner broken lines. Solid black squares, rectangles, and varying shapes represent buildings. Ruins are outlined. Rock features also will be shown in black.

Brown: Natural land features, such as earthbanks, gullies, depressions, dry ditches, pits, and knolls. Contour lines and form lines also are shown in brown.

Blue: Water features, including streams, rivers, ponds, lakes, oceans, springs, and swamps. Larger patches are ponds or lakes. A thin blue band is a stream, and a broader band is a river. A broken blue line means that a stream flows only some of the time. Swamps and marshes are shown with hatched blue lines.

Green: Vegetation. The shade of green may vary depending on the density of the ground cover under the trees: The darker the shade of green, the denser the ground vegetation. Dark green may reflect nearly impenetrable vegetation, and medium and light green shading could indicate vegetation that you could walk or slowly run through.

Yellow: Open terrain, where you can easily see the sun by looking up. Dark yellow is grass that is fairly short, lighter yellow is rough open terrain, and white dots on yellow is semiopen terrain with scattered trees and bushes throughout.

White: Open forest canopy with minimal ground vegetation. You can run fast through this terrain.

Red or purple: Indicates the layout of the orienteering course.

The International Orienteering Federation has adopted standard symbols to be used for orienteering maps, and these are used in the United States as well as the rest of the world.

Two factors are important when considering artificial features. First, they come and go. Don't depend on artificial features to find your way because they are the most likely to change with time. Many maps provide the date of compilation or revision. More recent maps are more likely to truly represent what is present. Second, artificial features may be represented on the map larger than they actually would be on the ground. Therefore, when measuring from a symbol that is exaggerated in size on a map, measure from the center of the symbol for the greatest accuracy.

Using a Map and Compass Together

In orienteering, you use the map and compass together as a unit, but the map is most important. You can navigate the course without a compass but not without a map.

Declination

The maps you are most likely to use on Scouting hikes or backpacking trips are drawn with their tops aimed at *true north*. Extend a map's boundaries far enough upward, and those lines will reach the north pole. You could say that these maps are made to speak the language of true north. However, compass needles do not point to true north. They are pulled toward *magnetic north,* an area in Canada more than a thousand miles away from the north pole. Compasses "speak" magnetic north, which is a different language from what most maps use.

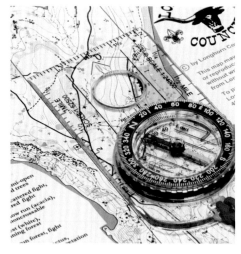

Arrows drawn in the bottom margin of many maps show the difference between true north and magnetic north. The true-north arrow points toward the north pole. The magnetic north arrow points toward magnetic north. The difference between true north and magnetic north, measured in degrees, is called *declination.* Because of declination, the compass needle will lie to the east or west of true north by as much as 20 degrees westerly in Maine and more than 30 degrees easterly in Alaska. Only in a thin strip from Lake Superior to Florida is there zero declination.

If you do not compensate for declination, you will not be able to find the actual direction between two points as related to the north and south of the landscape. The simplest solution is to convert the language of the map into the language of the compass. Do this by drawing magnetic north-south lines on the map by lining up a ruler against the magnetic north arrow and extending this line with a pencil to the top of the map. Draw parallel lines to this one, a ruler's width apart. This has already been done on all orienteering maps. Because they are drawn with tops aimed at magnetic north, compass readings can be obtained from or applied directly to these maps.

The difference between true north and magnetic north is called declination.

Magnetic Declination Map of the Continental United States

The map shown here is marked with lines along which compasses will show the same declination.

You can take a bearing from a map with magnetic north-south lines drawn on it by aligning the edge of the compass baseplate along the route of travel, making sure that the direction-of-travel arrow is pointing in the direction you intend to go. Rotate the bezel until the orienting arrow or north-south lines lie parallel to and in the same direction as the magnetic north-south lines on the map. Read the bearing directly opposite of the bearing index.

If the magnetic north-south lines are not drawn on the map, convert the language of the compass to that of the map. When you take a bearing from the map or apply it to the map, you must add or subtract the declination to the compass reading depending on whether the declination is easterly or westerly. Always add the number of degrees of error for west declination and subtract for east declination.

On the Sid Richardson Scout Ranch map, the compass edge is laid alongside the line from the hunter's stand at "A" and the northwest end of the cliff at "B." The bezel is turned until the north-south lines within the ring line up with the north arrow of the compass. Read the bearing from the index. The bearing is 244 degrees from "A" to "B." (Points "A" and "B" can be seen in the top photo on page 21.)

Orienting a Map With a Compass

Orienting a map means aligning it with the terrain. You can do this visually, but it is easier to make errors that way. A more accurate way of aligning the map and terrain is to use a compass. First, rotate the compass bezel until **N** or 360 degrees is lined up with the direction-of-travel arrow. Next, set the compass down on the map, with the compass edge along one of the north-south magnetic lines and the direction-of-travel arrow pointing north. Rotate the map and the compass until the compass needle matches the direction-of-travel arrow. The map is now oriented.

A quick field method of orienting the map is to hold the compass on the map and turn the map and compass so that the compass needle parallels or lines up with the north-south magnetic lines, with the north end of the needle toward the top of the map. Check the terrain around you to ensure that it matches what you see on the map. You can do this almost constantly while on a course and even when moving.

Measuring Distance on a Map

You can measure distance on a map by using a compass scale, a ruled compass edge, or any straight edge.

Using a Compass

Depending on the type of compass, a variety of scales may be marked along the edge of the baseplate. Ideally, one scale on the compass is the same as that on your map. For example, if your map has a scale of 1:24,000 and your compass has that scale on its baseplate, measuring distance is simple. Take the edge of the compass with the proper scale on it and connect the points for which the distance is desired. Simply read the distance directly from the scale. It is fairly common to find orienteering compasses with scales of 1:15,000, 1:24,000, or 1:62,500.

On a 1:15,000 scale, 1 inch on a map is approximately 1,300 feet or $1/4$ mile on the ground; on a 1:24,000 scale, 1 inch on a map is equal to 2,000 feet on the ground; and on a map with a scale of 1:62,500, 1 inch on the map is equal to 5,280 feet or about 1 mile on the ground.

Sometimes you might want to use the edge of the compass as a ruler, with inches on one side and millimeters on the other side of the baseplate. Measure the distance on the map with either scale and compare those distances with the distance rulers on the margin of the map. Read off the ground distance. Distance rulers on maps are generally in miles, kilometers, and feet.

Orienteering uses metric measurements, so you usually will use the kilometer/meter distance bar on the map.

Identifying Landmarks

With a compass and a map, you can identify a landmark that you can see from the ground if you know where you are on the map. Take a bearing to the object. Set the compass on the map with one edge of the baseplate touching your location. Point the N end of the housing toward the top of the map. Pivot the entire compass around your location until either the north-south lines in the compass housing or the orienting arrow parallels the north-south magnetic lines of the map. Extend a line from your location up into the map using the baseplate edge of the compass as a guide. Somewhere along that line is the landmark you wish to identify. Compare map, bearing, and actual terrain to locate and identify the feature in question.

Using a Straight Edge

You can easily calculate distances using a strip of paper or other straight edge. This works well on routes with several legs and routes that are not straight.

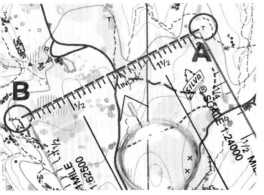

To measure the straight-line distance between the hunter's stand (A) and the northwest end of the cliff (B) on the Sid Richardson Scout Ranch map, place the straight edge along the line from "A" to "B." Make a mark on the edge of the paper at "A" and one at "B." Move the straight edge to the distance ruler on the map and measure the distance between the two marks. The distance is 585 meters.

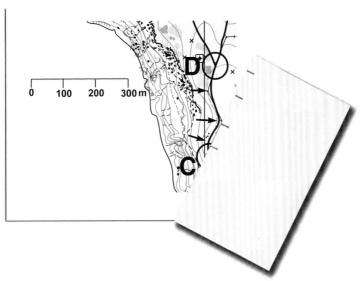

To figure a crooked-line distance between "C" and "D," lay a slip of paper on the map as in the illustration. Make a tick mark on the paper at "C" and at each bend in the route until you reach "D." You can determine the total distance by laying the piece of paper against the distance ruler and reading the result. The crooked-line distance in this example is 288 meters.

Judging Distance on the Ground

For some people, judging distance is the hardest part of orienteering. But you can make it easier with some preparation. One way of judging distance is by *pace-counting* or counting every time your right (or left) foot touches the ground over a given distance. Another method is to calculate the time it takes you to cover a predetermined distance. A standard length course for taking these measurements is 100 meters.

Setting Up a 100-Meter Pace-Measuring Course

Lay out a 100-meter course in a straight line using a tape measure. Clearly mark the beginning and the end of the course. It is best to lay out the course where terrain and vegetation are about the same throughout the entire course. This will help you determine more accurately your pace per 100 meters for a given type of terrain or vegetation.

If you will be moving through a variety of terrain and vegetation while orienteering, it is best to determine a 100-meter pace for each type of area in which you will travel. This could mean setting up several 100-meter pace courses. When choosing an area to set up courses, look for places that have a number of 100-meter-long blocks with differing conditions. This will save time in the process of learning your pace count.

If the terrain is too mixed, the value you get for the pace count will be less accurate for any single condition.

Tip: Remember, you are growing rapidly in this stage of your life. Your pace will change as you grow and start taking longer strides. Remeasure your pace frequently.

Walking Pace/Time

Every time orienteers switch from walking to running or the reverse, they must mentally adjust the pace and time as well.

Once you have laid out the course, start at the beginning and walk the length of it, counting the number of paces and recording the time it takes you to reach the end. This is your walking pace and time per 100 meters. You will get a more accurate measure if you walk the course two or more times and then divide the total paces and minutes by the total meters walked. This is particularly important if the course is on uneven ground.

Running Pace/Time

Foot speed is important in orienteering, especially for competitive orienteering. As your stride lengthens, the distance you cover increases. So the number of paces per 100 meters will decrease, as will the time it takes you to cover that distance.

Measuring your running pace and time is exactly the same as measuring your walking pace. Because this is much more active, it is even more important that you run the course several times to get a true measure.

Uphill and Downhill Pace/Time

Your stride will shorten as you move uphill, so the number of paces and the time to cover 100 meters will be more than on level terrain.

You can get downhill measurements on the same course you use for the uphill by traveling in the opposite direction. Gravity wants to pull the downhill walker or runner along at a faster clip. Your stride will lengthen and the number of paces and time per 100 meters will decrease.

Vegetation Pace/Time

The runnability of vegetation can vary from impenetrable (called *fight* by orienteers), walkable, slowly runnable, and runnable. These conditions may be indicated on maps made especially for orienteering (see the legend of the Sid Richardson Scout Ranch map). Other maps indicate only that vegetation is present, so each meter you traverse can be a surprise—sometimes pleasant, sometimes not. However, you probably will have a general idea what the vegetation will be like in your area.

You can make more accurate pace estimates by calculating paces and times on several 100-meter courses through typical vegetation for your area.

Some orienteering meets use electronic punching to record competitors' times.

Competitive Orienteering

There are two major forms of orienteering competition: *score orienteering* and *cross-country orienteering* (also called free or point-to-point orienteering). There are a number of variations of each type.

Score Orienteering

In score orienteering competitions, many *controls,* or checkpoints, are placed in an area of 1 to 2 kilometers around the starting point, which is also the finish line. The number of controls may vary. Each one can have a point value. Controls that are farthest from the start or hardest to find are awarded a high point value; those near the start and easy to find get lower values.

Competitors have a set time to find as many controls as they can and earn as large a point total as possible. They may visit the controls in any order they wish. The course is designed so that they cannot possibly find all the controls in the time allowed. A penalty of 1 point is subtracted from a competitor's total for every 10 seconds he is overdue at the finish. In team events, this penalty can be changed to 5 points for every minute late. The highest score wins.

In score orienteering, there is no reward for arriving at the finish ahead of time. Competitors must judge the time well and know their own ability at running and map reading in relation to time and distance. This is the best way to introduce orienteering to a group of beginners because it is an equal test for the strong runner and map reader and for the novice.

Team Competition

Team competition is an ideal competition for Scouts when they become good at orienteering. Prizes can be awarded for the best individual competitor and the best team.

Score orienteering can be run as a team competition. Each team is given marked maps and a score sheet that describes all the controls and shows their point values. The team captain notes the length of time that the team has to complete the course. He then assigns controls to each member of the team, giving the harder ones to the best members of the team and the easier ones to the weakest members. He may send team members off in pairs. The competitors find the controls assigned to them, note the code letter on each control, and report back to their leader. The team cannot hand in its score sheet with the code letters written in until all members of the team have returned.

Another way to run this event is to have only the best scores for each team count toward the team total. This number is at the discretion of event organizers. Each member starts at a different time so that he or she cannot help anyone else. The team's score is the total of the best individual scores.

Variations on Score Orienteering

In **night orienteering,** competitors use lights on the course, and the controls often are marked with reflective tape. In **ski orienteering,** skis and ski trails are used. There is a well-established international competition in ski orienteering. **ROGAINE (Rugged Outdoor Group Activity Involving Navigation and Endurance)** events last a long time—6, 12, 24, or 48 hours. Generally, competitors must work with a partner or group. These variations also can be used for cross-country orienteering.

Cross-Country, Free, or Point-to-Point Orienteering

In cross-country orienteering, every competitor must visit the same controls in numerical order, and as quickly as possible. This form of orienteering is a challenge in route choice and stamina. Controls, usually eight to 24, will be marked on competitors' maps with numbered circles. All features where controls are placed will be clearly described on a *control description sheet* that each competitor gets along with the map. Each control will have a unique code letter or number.

CONTROL MAP FOR YELLOW
(ADVANCED BEGINNER) LEVEL COURSE

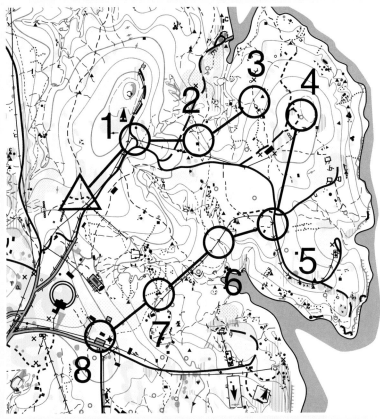

Study the cross-country course shown here. The descriptive clues on the control description sheet for this contest would look like this:

1. Road bend

2. Building northeast outside corner

3. Trail junction stream

4. Special artificial feature

5. Trail junction pipeline

6. Pipeline crossing stream

7. Northeastern boulder cluster

8. Building southwest outside corner

In line

orienteering,

competitors

start at different

times so that

they can't follow

in another's

footsteps.

Cross-country courses are age- and skill-graded and can vary in length. A junior or beginner's course may be only 1.5 kilometers long, while a championship course can be up to 14 kilometers. Course levels, indicated by color, progress from novice to expert: white (beginner), yellow (advanced beginner), orange (intermediate), and brown, green, red, and blue (advanced). Long-course orienteering courses are up to twice as long as the standard course of the same level. The winner in each age and course level is the fastest competitor who has all the correct control punches.

Line Orienteering

Line orienteering is organized like the cross-country event, with one major difference: No controls are marked on the master map, only a route. The route sometimes follows trails. At other times it goes through woods on a direct bearing. Eventually it returns to the starting location.

Competitors must copy this route exactly on their own maps and follow it as fast as possible by accurate map reading. If they are accurate, they will find controls along the route. There is a time penalty of 10 to 15 minutes for each missed control. The fastest person around the course with the highest number of controls found wins.

Relay Orienteering

Relay orienteering is the most popular team competition. All the rules for cross-country orienteering apply to relay orienteering with one addition: A competitor runs only one loop. The number of loops in the relay depends on the number of members on a team.

The first team member runs to the master map and finds only the controls of his own loop marked on the map. The first runner will be given a *baton*—an identity disk on a cord to hang around his neck. Sometimes the map or the control card is the baton. The runner hands it to the next runner on the team when he has completed his loop. The next member of the team then does his loop and so forth until all members have finished their loops and the team has completed the course.

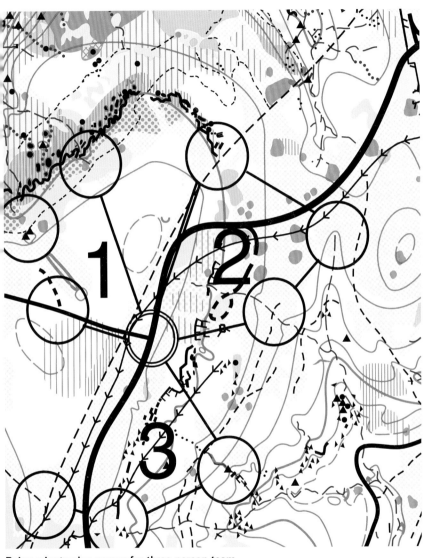

Relay orienteering course for three-person team

Route Orienteering

Participants in orienteering events carry a *control card,* which they punch or stamp at each control to prove that they have been there.

In route orienteering, a course is marked on the ground with colored streamers so that it is simple to move from one streamer to the next. The course may meander through woods and across fields until it eventually finishes where it started. At varying distances along the course, yellow flags are placed beside reasonably obvious features. There also is a series of blue flags. Each blue flag is beside a sighting stick with a fore site and a rear site at objects such as a house, a windmill, or a corner of a wood no farther than 1,500 meters away. An official waits at each flag.

Competitors are given some pins and a map stapled to cardboard. The only thing marked on the map is the location of the start. The start time of the competitor is noted, and he is sent down the course.

Competitors must count their paces and check their location the entire time they are on the course. When they see a yellow flag, they make a pinprick on their maps at the exact location of the yellow flag. The pricks must be accurate; the official checks the pin mark and gives a two-minute penalty for every millimeter the pinprick is off. When competitors reach a blue flag, they make a pinprick on their maps for the object at which the sighting stick is pointing. Competitors must know their own location to correctly pinpoint the object's location. Again, a two-minute penalty for each millimeter of error is added to the total time around the course. The course may be 2 to 4 kilometers long with eight yellow and three blue flags.

The judge at the finish has a template showing the exact locations of all controls. Laying the template on top of the competitor's map will reveal any errors in marking.

Window and Corridor Orienteering

In corridor orienteering, a variation of point-to-point orienteering, competitors are given a map with only a narrow strip of terrain visible. If only the control points are visible, it is called window orienteering. These types of competition place a premium on compass skills and the ability to figure out the terrain without seeing the "big picture."

General Orienteering Rules

Orienteering USA is the ruling body for sanctioned orienteering events in the United States. Its rule book is comprehensive and addresses the technicalities of holding an event, as well as conduct that is expected of the participants. A few general rules are provided below, but for detailed information, it is best to consult the rule book or to contact the OUSA.

1. Competitors who have prior knowledge of the course that will give them an unfair advantage should not participate. Investigation of the course before an event is forbidden.

2. The use of any navigational aid other than a compass is prohibited, including GPS (global positioning system) units, altimeters, and pedometers. Competitors may use only a compass and the map provided by the organizer.

3. Competitors cannot use outside help nor collaborate with other competitors.

4. It is unfair to profit from the skills of the other competitors.

5. Competitors must move over the course as quietly as possible, so as not to disturb or aid fellow competitors.

6. All participants should be aware of how danger areas are identified and avoid them.

7. It is a competitor's duty to help anyone who is injured.

8. Competitors must not damage competition terrain.

9. Competitors must close all gates and barriers that they may have opened.

10. Competitors must stay out of yards, gardens, planted fields, limited-access roads, railway corridors, and areas marked "Out of Bounds." The only exception to this is if permission has been given in the race instructions.

11. If competitors have not completed the course by the designated closing time, they must report to the race authorities at the finish line and turn in control cards and maps. They must not remain on the course past the competition close. Competitors must never leave the course area without informing race officials.

Source: Adapted from "Selected Rules of Orienteering," a summary by Joe Scarborough, in *Orienteering: The Sport of Navigating with Map and Compass,* by Steven Boga, Stackpole Books, 1997.

Memory Orienteering

In a memory orienteering competition, competitors are shown only one leg of the course at a time, and they must memorize it before setting off for the control point. The course is completed through a series of memorization and movement legs. This is excellent practice in training the mind to learn information quickly and accurately. This skill is essential to be competitive in orienteering, in that it is directly related to speed.

Trail Orienteering

Trail orienteering is a competitive form of national and international orienteering that is suitable for people with physical disabilities. Participants use high-quality trails to get near the controls, where they must determine the correct control from several choices.

International Control Description Symbols and Sheets

Competitors get a control description or clue sheet and map before or at the start of an orienteering event. For beginners' courses, the clues are given in symbols and written out in words, but for intermediate and advanced competitors, the clues are given in a table format with symbols. A lot of information can be given, and the best competitors read carefully to get as much information as possible.

To promote international competition, the IOF has standardized the maps and symbols used. This makes it possible for orienteers to compete in events in any country, even without understanding that country's language. The symbols are easy to learn. You can guess what most mean without a description.

Column	A	B	C	D	E	F	G	H	
	Yellow			1.64K			70m		
	Start	△			Y				Start path junction
	1	121		/	(				Road bend
	2	114		▬			⌐		Building northeast outside corner
	3	101			X	\\\			Path crossing ditch
	4	159		○					Special item
	5	132			Y	⚞			Path junction pipeline
	6	164		\\\	X	⚞			Ditch crossing pipeline
	7	166		▲					Boulder cluster
	8	191		▬			·		Building southwest outside corner
	○				136		→○			136m marked route to finish

Control description sheet for yellow course

Examine the sample control description sheet shown here. The top of the sheet shows the level of competition (yellow), the course distance in meters (1.64 kilometers), and the meters of vertical climb along the route (70 meters).

Column A shows the control points in the order they are visited, numbers 1 through 8. Column B shows the control codes used in the competition, followed by a "description" of each control's location in the rest of the columns. (See the international control description symbols shown on the following pages.) The last line describes how competitors will approach the finish from the last control—in the example, a 136-meter marked route to the finish.

International Control Description Symbols

Column C: Which Feature (of any similar ones)?

↓	Southern
↗	Northeastern
÷	Upper
÷	Lower
ǂ	Middle

Column D: The Control Feature

ᴍᴍ	Steep bank
☺	Quarry
⊞	Earthbank, dam
⏗	Terrace
⏉	Spur
⢾	Rib
∧	Re-entrant
⋀	Gully
⬚	Dry ditch
○	Hill
●	Knoll
)(	Saddle
⊖	Depression
∪	Small depression
∨	Pit
⊓	Cliff, crag
☀	Bare rock
⅄	Cave
▲	Boulder
⣀	Boulder field
▦	Stony ground
▲▲	Cairn/stone pile

Column D (continued)

][	Narrow passage (between cliffs)
⊚	Lake
ᴗ	Pond
∨	Water hole
⌇	Stream
⌇	Ditch
≡	Marsh
⁼	Small marsh
⊡	Firm ground
⍥	Well
⌇	Spring
⋰	Narrow marsh
⌇	Seasonal watercourse
◇	Open land, field
⬚	Semiopen land
⬦	Forest corner
○	Clearing
✳	Thicket
▨	Felled area
⋱	Vegetation boundary
⟁	Copse
⌁	Hedge
⊬	Linear thicket
/	Road
⁄	Path
⋰	Narrow ride
⟋	Wall
⟋	Fence
⫽	Footbridge

Column D (continued)

- Building
- Ruin
- Tower
- Power line
- Power line pylon/pole
- Shooting platform
- Fodder rack
- Rock pillar
- Single tree
- Salt lick
- Root stock
- Boundary stone
- Charcoal burning ground
- Anthill
- Broken ground
- Special feature
- Special feature

Column E: Details of Appearance

- Shallow
- Deep
- Overgrown
- Open
- Rocky
- Marshy
- Sandy
- Coniferous
- Deciduous
- Ruined or collapsed

Column F: Dimensions of the Feature

5.5	Height in meters
7x5	Size in meters (length/width)
1.5/2.0	Height of object on slope

Column G: Location of the Marker

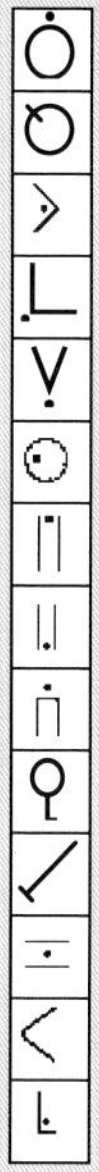

- North side
- Northwest edge
- East corner (inside)
- Southwest corner
- Southern tip
- Western part
- Upper part (head)
- Lower part (foot)
- On top of
- Southern foot
- Southwest end
- Between
- Bend
- At the foot

Column H: Other Information

- Refreshments
- Radio control
- Manned control
- First aid

Orienteering Techniques

Orienteers use a number of techniques to choose their routes along a course.

Handrails

Handrails are linear features along the leg of a course that lead you in the direction you want to go and provide easier travel, continuous direction, and a more accurate position. Orienteers' handrails can be either natural or artificial features such as

Even the most skilled orienteer should always be looking for navigational handrails in the terrain.

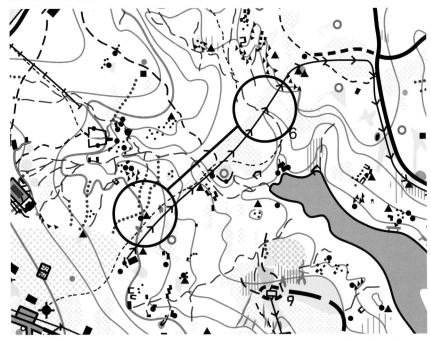

In this illustration, the orienteer follows the pipeline handrail almost directly to the control location.

streams, trails, roads, fences, and power lines. More obscure handrails might be ridge lines, valleys, tree lines, forest fire burns, or avalanche scars.

Beginners' courses rely heavily on handrails to help the novice get to each control. The route for the easiest courses may actually go right down a trail or road—the handrail. As the orienteer's skills develop and the courses become more difficult, handrails become less obvious, but the terrain will have usable handrails if the map reader is skilled enough to pick them out from the details.

Collecting, Check-Off, and Catching Features

Always look around and take note of the features you pass as you move toward the next control. There may be some obvious features along the route, such as a large pond or small lake, that will help send you in the right direction. These are *collecting features,* which lie *between* you and the control.

Equally important but less obvious are *check-off features,* which you will see along the way. You can constantly verify your position by making a mental note as you pass the features and moving your thumb along the map as you go.

A *catching feature* lies *beyond* the control. This term makes sense if you think of a catching feature as a landmark that warns you that you have actually passed the control. The feature catches you!

Attack Point

An *attack point* is a large, easily recognized feature that is near the control. The attack point helps you determine your exact location and reach the control. From the attack point, you can use precise navigation, such as an accurate bearing and pace counting, to carefully zero in on the control. The route from the attack point to the control may be so obvious, or so restricted, that you might not even have to take a compass bearing. Generally, orienteering relies more heavily on the map than the compass.

In using collecting points, check-off, and catching features, remember that features on older maps may have long since disappeared.

Aiming Off or Offset Technique

If a control or attack point is on a linear feature, such as a road, it can be more efficient and safer to deliberately aim off to one side of the straight line that heads to the feature. If you arrive at the linear feature and do not see the control, you will then know which way to turn to find it.

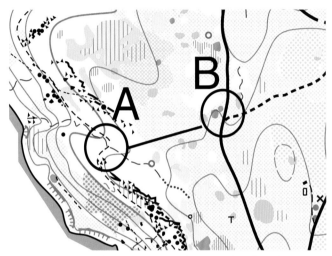

In this map, it would be easy to reach the road and not be sure what direction the control lies. To prevent this, you can deliberately aim a few meters south of the control so you know to turn north when you get to the road.

Reading Ahead

Keep a clear mental picture of the terrain that you will pass through. Read the map every few seconds, think beyond your location, and plan ahead. The best way to practice reading ahead is to take time at the beginning of the course and after each control to make sure you understand what the map is telling you. Do not move until you are sure. It is just as important to keep oriented every moment while you are traveling and to keep an eye on what lies ahead. Keep your map out

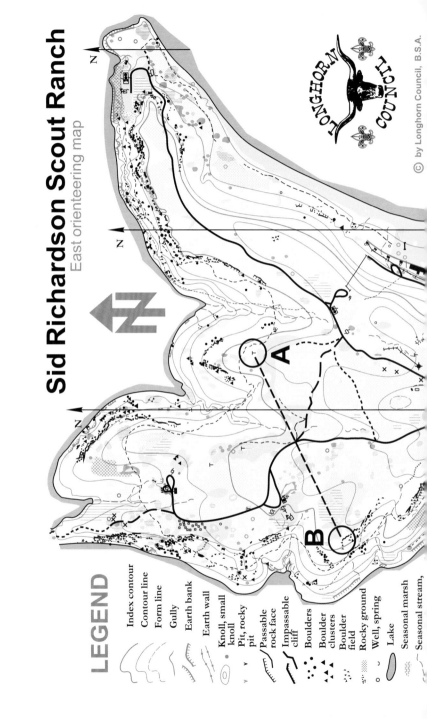

Sid Richardson Scout Ranch

East orienteering map

© by Longhorn Council, B.S.A.

LONGHORN COUNCIL

LEGEND

- Index contour
- Contour line
- Form line
- Gully
- Earth bank
- Earth wall
- Knoll, small knoll
- Pit, rocky pit
- Passable rock face
- Impassable cliff
- Boulders
- Boulder clusters
- Boulder field
- Rocky ground
- Well, spring
- Lake
- Seasonal marsh
- Seasonal stream,

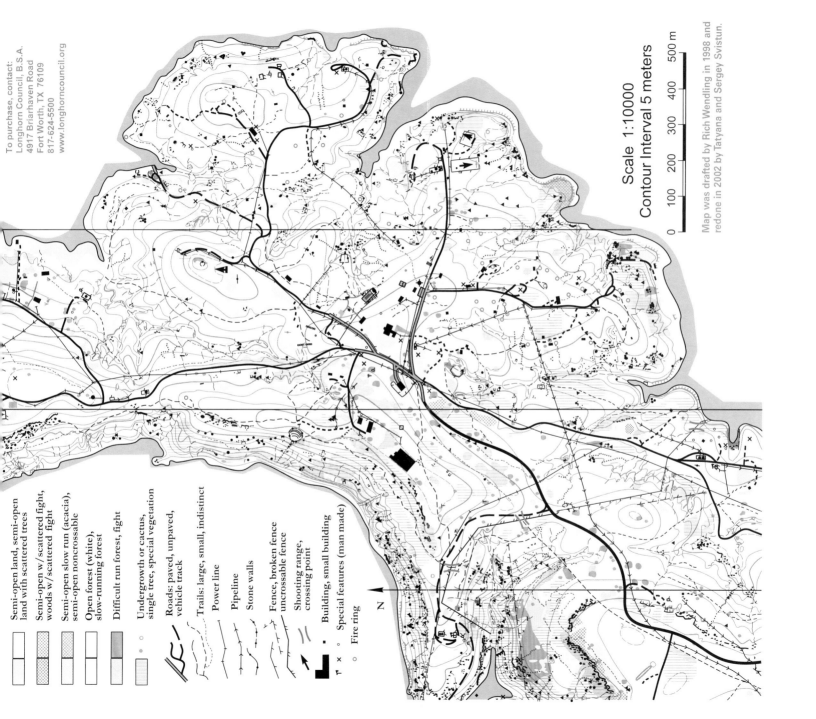

To purchase, contact:
Longhorn Council, B.S.A.
4917 Briarhaven Road
Fort Worth, TX 76109
817-624-5500
www.longhorncouncil.org

Scale 1:10000
Contour Interval 5 meters

0   100   200   300   400   500 m

Map was drafted by Rich Wendling in 1998 and
redone in 2002 by Tatyana and Sergey Svistun.

Semi-open land, semi-open
land with scattered trees

Semi-open w/ scattered fight,
woods w/ scattered fight

Semi-open slow run (acacia),
semi-open noncrossable

Open forest (white),
slow-running forest

Difficult run forest, fight

Undergrowth or cactus,
single tree, special vegetation

Roads: paved, unpaved,
vehicle track

Trails: large, small, indistinct

Power line

Pipeline

Stone walls

Fence, broken fence
uncrossable fence

Shooting range,
crossing point

Building, small building

Special features (man made)

Fire ring

N

and refer to it often. Make sure that what you are seeing on the ground matches what the map tells you should be there. If you find this is not the case, then either you are reading the map wrong or you have strayed from your intended course.

Contouring

Sometimes, the direct up-and-over or down-and-up route between controls is not the best. Take a few seconds to calculate the elevation where you are standing and the elevation at the next control. Are they roughly the same? If they are, it may be best to follow a route that stays at the same elevation. That route is plainly marked on the map—the contour line!

Following the contour line is called *contouring,* and it is often the most efficient path of travel between two points in rough terrain.

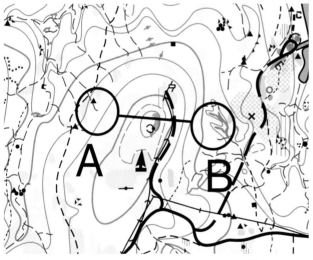

In this example, a person who is contouring would follow a route that is level or downhill. The direct route would mean a climb of 10 to 15 meters (33 to 50 feet). Although the distance to contour is greater, the effort expended is less.

You should consider contouring even if there is quite a difference in the length of the straight-line route versus the contour-line route. The route may look faster as the crow flies, but that may be deceptive.

Relocation

Contouring is also useful for avoiding obstacles. Trail builders do this all the time. If they did not, nobody would want to go hiking!

When a person is lost or potentially lost, whether on a road in a city, deep in a complex cave, in the wilderness, or on an orienteering course, *the best thing to do is stop.* The worst thing to do is to keep moving, because the problem will not correct itself; it will get worse. And time lost in correcting the problem will skyrocket.

If you don't know where you are, stop and relocate. Find a definite feature that you can correctly locate. This should be relatively easy to do if you took the time before the start to compare the map with the terrain and make a mental note of *relocation features* such as lakes and ponds, where two streams intersect, or perhaps a bridge where a stream goes under a road. Almost anything will work, but it must be prominent enough so that you do not confuse it with other features. If you mix up relocation sites, you will really be lost and might have to retrace part of the route to find a recognizable point.

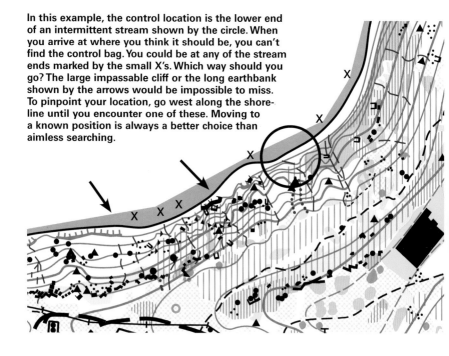

In this example, the control location is the lower end of an intermittent stream shown by the circle. When you arrive at where you think it should be, you can't find the control bag. You could be at any of the stream ends marked by the small X's. Which way should you go? The large impassable cliff or the long earthbank shown by the arrows would be impossible to miss. To pinpoint your location, go west along the shoreline until you encounter one of these. Moving to a known position is always a better choice than aimless searching.

Rough Versus Fine Orienteering

The search for the next control point in an orienteering problem often can be divided into two distinct phases: the rough orienteering phase and the fine orienteering phase.

In the *rough phase,* you are moving in broadly defined directions toward a collection point found on the map. This is the time for covering a lot of ground quickly. You will not be in danger of missing the control during this phase because the control will not be close at hand yet.

Rough orienteering the whole way will cause a lot of aimless thrashing about, but fine orienteering all the way will waste valuable time. As orienteering involves a combination of speed and accuracy, so, too, does each leg of an orienteering course.

Orienteers in complex terrain are always checking behind them as they go forward. This gives them the option of relocating to familiar terrain.

Once you reach the chosen collection point, it is time to switch to *fine orienteering.* Locate yourself precisely, and determine where you are in relation to the control. Form a plan that will accurately lead you to the control. This may involve using handrails, attack points, and compass bearings. Proceed to the control as quickly as possible, but remember that in this phase accuracy is the primary goal.

Route Choice

Orienteering allows competitors to choose their route around the course, introducing an element of skill that complements physical fitness. When confronted with many possible routes, you should consider the following:

- Terrain barriers or obstacles, vegetation
- Off-limit areas
- Artificial features and the presence of landmarks, handrails, collecting features, catching features, and attack points
- Your level of physical fitness
- The adequacy of your clothing for certain routes

Moving through thick vegetation may take up to 10 times as long as moving along an open trail.

As the courses progress from the (novice) white level to the advanced beginner yellow, intermediate orange, and advanced brown, green, red, and blue courses, better route-finding skills become desirable, and then essential. The most advanced courses may have many options for reaching the control but only one or two really good ones.

Vegetation

FIGHT! This word is the orienteer's expression for vegetation that is nearly impenetrable. If you see fight on a map, or its color equivalent—dark green—you are in for "vegetable combat" if you try to go through it. It probably is chock-full with

undergrowth and deadfall. Unless the proposed route is marked runnable or is light green or, even better, white on the map, you should consider another route. A 1,000-meter detour might leave you fresh and smiling at the control and relieved that you did not take the 100-meter shortcut that left another orienteer scratched and haggard. He has been in a fight, while you were just having fun!

Elevation

No matter how sweet a route looks otherwise, if a hill sits between you and the control, it will slow your time. How much? That depends on the steepness of the hill, but a good rule of thumb is that 15 meters of climb is equal to running about 100 meters on flat ground. So a 45-meter hill will be equivalent to running 300 meters. If you can contour around the hill in less than 300 meters, then go around rather than over. Sometimes the next control is situated at a higher elevation than the last. In this case you have no option but to go up.

Steps in Choosing a Route

Route choice will be simplified if each time you set out for a control you:

1. Note the exact location of the control on the map and read its description from the description sheet.

2. Choose an attack point (if the control is not placed in an obvious position) very close to a feature that you can easily recognize— a bridge, a trail junction, power lines over a path, a corner of a forest.

3. Look at the direct route from your present position to the attack point. See whether it will be easy to follow on a compass bearing.

4. Look to the left and right of the direct route and see whether there is an easier and quicker route. An indirect route may require less hill climbing and pushing through dense woods.

5. Take the fastest route to the attack point.

6. Run as fast as possible to the attack point, using collecting features to find the way.

7. Take an accurate compass bearing (if necessary) from the attack point to the control.

8. Measure the exact distance on the map from the attack point to the control.

9. Walk or jog accurately on a compass bearing, counting the paces until you find the control.

Once you master the basic map reading and compass skills, the winning edge often will come down to route choice. And this skill depends a lot on experience.

Route Choice Examples

Study the four points on the route choice illustration. The obvious route from the start triangle to point No. 1 is along the road. Course setters often will make the first control easy so competitors can get used to the map.

You have a choice to make from No. 1 to No. 2. The easiest route goes along the main road and then north at the trail to the building. A more direct route is along the power line and across the secondary road to the boulders, where you can take a bearing directly to the building. It is shorter, but vegetation may slow your progress.

It is a difficult choice from No. 2 to No. 3. The easy but long way is south on the trail, east on the road, northeast on the secondary road, and then north along the trail. You will always know exactly where you are on the map. While the direct route uses a bearing and is much shorter, you must cross two streambeds and vegetation.

From No. 3 to No. 4 the choice is easier. A direct course is probably faster, as the woods are open (white color—runnable) and the road you will cross is a great collecting feature that you can't miss. In addition, the feature is near the top of a hill, making it easy to find. Going south on the trail and then northeast on the road is easy travel but twice as far.

Examine the rest of the sample yellow course in the "Competitive Orienteering" section. Decide which route you would take between the remaining points. There usually is not one correct answer; nevertheless, route choice is *the* key to successful orienteering.

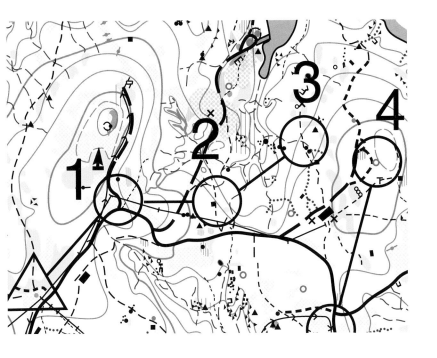

Setting Up a Competition

When you take a turn at setting up an orienteering course and competition, you will see the sport in a different light. As a competitor your main goal on race day is to decipher the course and move around it as quickly and accurately as possible. As an organizer, you must begin thinking about the race weeks in advance. *When? Where? How?* and *Who?* are all questions you will have to address in setting up a competition.

When are you going to put on the competition? Maybe during camp or at a jamboree, on a summer evening, or on a weekend. You will have to choose a date and time, and let prospective participants know about it.

The *where* of the course will be a site that is both challenging and safe, and a site for which a map is available. Consider city parks and state parks, as well as areas controlled by the BSA. National forest areas also might be a possibility.

How will the competition be conducted? Will it be a cross-country or a score event? How difficult will the competition be? How long will the course be? Will the start and finish be at the same place? Will winners receive awards? What sort of refreshments will you provide for finishers?

Who will compete? Will it be for your patrol only, or will you invite the entire troop? Maybe it will be a team event where patrols compete against one another.

These are just some of the details that need to be worked out in setting up an orienteering competition. To plan the best event possible, a team of Scouts and leaders working closely together probably will be needed. Maybe your patrol could put on the competition for another patrol and then the other patrol could set up a competition for yours. This way, each group experiences the thrill of competing but also comes to understand orienteering in a much deeper way.

Be sure that you always get permission beforehand from the landowner, whether that be a private individual or government agency.

First-Aid Equipment

A comprehensive first-aid kit should be available at the start and finish—two kits if these areas are separated. A patrol or troop first-aid kit will treat a range of injuries. The most common types of injuries will be foot injuries, strains and sprains, and cuts and bruises. Blister treatments, ice and support bandages, and other bandages and dressing should be available. Additionally, each participant may carry a personal first-aid kit for those small injuries that might occur away from the start and finish areas. (See also the chapter "Orienteering First Aid.")

Equipment

For a good orienteering competition, the following equipment and materials are necessary:

- Competitors' maps for each competitor
- Control cards, one per competitor
- Two recorder's sheets
- Control description sheets, one for each competitor
- Two time clocks
- Start sign
- Finish sign
- Rope with pegs to make a finishing tunnel
- Results board
- One control marker or punch per control point

- Extra compasses
- Whistle, for starting
- First-aid kit
- Colored tape or ribbon for marking administrative lanes, and routes from the start to the master map and from the last control point to the finish

If the course maps are not preprinted, you will need to mount three to five master maps on card tables so that each competitor can copy the course to a blank map.

Safety

Safety is the No. 1 concern for all orienteering competitions. Strive to prevent injury by stressing that competitors must make wise decisions. At least one member of the team putting on the competition should be trained in first aid. A plan should be in place in the event of a serious injury, including how to contact medical personnel and facilities. All competitors should be briefed on safety procedures. When appropriate, they should write this information on their maps.

> The *First Aid* merit badge pamphlet and the *Boy Scout Handbook* cover basic first aid for a variety of situations. Portions of those books have been condensed in the "Orienteering First Aid" chapter.

Safety Lane

A well-laid-out course should have a *safety lane* where competitors may go if hurt, too tired to finish, or lost. Usually the safety lane is on the boundary of the course. It could be a major feature like a fence, power line, clear-cut, or road that bisects the area. All a competitor needs to do is set a standard bearing on the compass and follow it until he reaches the lane. After the competition, if some competitors have not returned, the officials drive along the boundaries of the course to pick up orienteers who have retreated to the safety lane.

On the Sid Richardson Scout Ranch map, the main road running the length of the ranch is used as the safety lane. On the sample yellow course in the "Competitive Orienteering" section, the safety lane is located west to the main camp road.

Final Return Time

All orienteering events must have a final return time. Competitors must return to the finish by then, regardless of whether they have completed the course. Failure to do so will result in a search being mounted. Competitors should have a watch and a signaling device as part of their basic emergency gear.

Location

The framework of all orienteering courses is the competition site and its map. Each must be considered before any detailed planning of an orienteering event is possible.

Area With an Existing Map

Even more than the compass, the map is the foundation of orienteering. Without it, there is no course. There are two options: Find an area that has an existing map, or make a map of the area yourself.

The first option is easiest. You may be surprised to discover the number of areas that have been mapped. Probably the maps most available to the general public are the USGS 7.5-minute quadrangle topographic maps, which have a scale of 1:24,000, where 1 inch on the map equals 2,000 feet on the ground. The topographic features of these maps may not be found on other maps. These are available through local suppliers or from the USGS itself. Other government agencies such as the Forest Service, National Park Service, the Bureau of Land Management, state geological surveys, state park and recreation agencies, and county and city parks departments will have maps of varying usefulness. Private property will be the least likely to have been mapped, unless a government agency did it.

 From World War II through the late 1980s, the USGS made more than 57,000 7.5-minute maps covering the 48 mainland states. Today, the USGS produces more than 80,000 maps. These include the 7.5-minute series and topographic maps at smaller scales, maps of U.S. possessions and territories and of Antarctica, special maps of national parks and monuments, and geologic and hydrologic maps.

Because of the increasing popularity of the sport of orienteering, more and more maps designed specifically for orienteering are available, such as the centerfold map of Sid Richardson Scout Ranch. Such maps are often large-scale maps, typically 1:15,000 or even 1:10,000, and have legends and colors especially relating to orienteering. If you plan to run a competition in an urban area, it would be worthwhile to ask local orienteering groups whether maps are available of the area you intend to use.

Lastly, some cartography companies will create maps to your specifications.

Area Without an Existing Map

Creating your own map sounds like a lot of hard work, but actually, it is not that hard, and it can be a lot of fun, too. Before you start the mapping process, you should have a pretty good idea of how long the course will be, the direction of travel, the locations of the controls, and the relationship of the finish to the start.

It is always wise to field-check anything included on your new map—riverbeds change, structures collapse, roads come and go, homes are built, ponds are constructed, swamps are drained, etc.

The easiest low-tech way to create a course map is to take an existing map, such as a USGS topographic map, and add more detail to it. This detail could include IOF symbols, IOF terminology, orienteering vegetation colors, and magnetic north lines. You can even change the scale of the old map to one that conforms better with IOF standards. You can make the changes right on the old map.

Most orienteering maps are made with a computer program called OCAD. You can download a demonstration version online. It is fully operational but limited in capacity. This is the standard for today's orienteering maps.

Another way of converting a USGS topographic map is to lay tracing paper or clear plastic over the old map, tracing what you want from the old map and adding detail specific to orienteering.

Aerial photos and satellite photos are available for free on the Internet, such as the USGS Web site. Be sure to get your parent's permission before down-loading anything from the Internet.

Creating a map from scratch requires a little preliminary scouting of the area. Take a half-day to thoroughly familiarize yourself with things such as the terrain, vegetation, natural and artificial features, hazards, and potential control sites. Take a small notebook along to record information about the site that you want to remember as you make your map. Understand the general lay of the land. This will begin to give you ideas about how and where you can lay out the course.

Take a few minutes after your reconnaissance (inspection) of the area to plot a rough course in your notebook. You will modify and fine-tune this working model of your course when you return to map the area. Unless you plan your course, you will waste time mapping areas that the course does not use.

This little bit of planning allows you to show up at the start point, ready to map. Take a blank sheet of paper on a clipboard, several sharpened pencils (working in pencil allows easy changes), a ruler, and an orienteering compass. Use the ruler to help you draw parallel lines on the paper to represent magnetic north lines, in effect making the sheet of paper speak the language of the compass. The top of each line points to magnetic north. Indicate this on the top of the paper.

Two other questions remain to be answered before setting off: What will the scale of your map be, and where should you put the starting point on the blank sheet of paper? Because of your preliminary work, these questions should be relatively easy to answer. For instance, if the roughed-out course goes north, west, south, and then back east, it would be best to place the starting point on the paper in the lower right-hand (southeast) corner. This allows the course to remain on the paper. Mark an X on the paper to indicate the start.

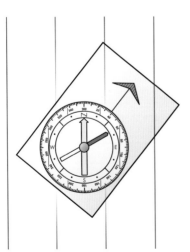

The map's scale also will determine whether it will cover one or more sheets of paper. Generally, it is best to use only one sheet. A scale of 1:1,200 will allow a closed traverse of about 1,200 meters to fit onto a single sheet, while a scale of 1:2,400 will double the terrain that you can fit onto the page but will decrease the map's detail.

You are now ready to begin mapping.

1. Standing at the start (which you should mark so that you can return to it easily), take a compass bearing to the first point.

2. Plot this bearing onto the paper by placing the edge of the compass on the X and rotating the compass until the orienting arrow or the north-south lines of the compass are parallel to the magnetic north lines on the paper.

3. Using the edge of the compass, draw a line onto the paper. The point lies somewhere along this line. To determine where, walk to it as you count your paces. If you have practiced counting your paces, you will be able to figure how far the point is and place it accurately onto your line. Put a small X here. You will take the next bearing from this point.

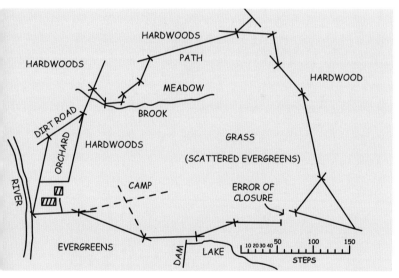

This process provides only a "stick figure" map. Add detail along the bearing lines by noting and sketching in natural and artificial features as you move along. You can reach a fair level of accuracy by pacing off distances and taking rough compass bearings. To locate a feature more precisely, take a bearing on it from two known points on the route. The feature is located at the intersection of the two bearings.

Walk around the intended course taking bearings and plotting them onto the map until you return either to the starting point or to a separate finish.

You now have a rough field map of the area. Tidy it up and add as much detail as you like. Particularly important are a scale relating distance to pace and a magnetic north arrow. You can add symbols for certain terrain features and color to show vegetation. Make sure you explain the symbols and colors in a map legend. Date your map, as features change with time. Give it a name, and put your name on it as mapmaker.

Once you have the area map in hand, whether it be a preexisting one or one you have made, make individual maps for each contestant and several master maps. The master map

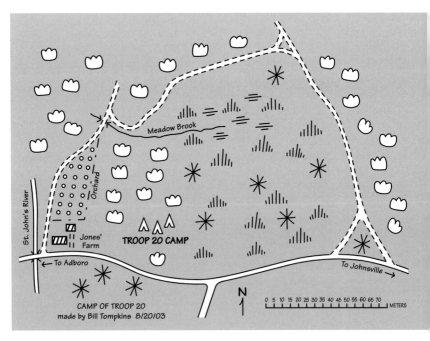

You probably will not be able to place contour lines on your map. If the area you are mapping will be used extensively for orienteering, you could research and use computer software that allows you to create topographic maps.

The assembly area should be large enough to hold all competitors and officials at the same time.

will be available for all contestants to study but not carry with them. It will contain all the information you wish to give out. The individual maps do not need to contain everything that is on the master.

Competition Site

Besides the course, the location for your orienteering event will require a meeting place for contestants, officials, and spectators, and areas for checking pace, consulting the master map, and reporting to race officials for the send-off and finish. The finish should complement the other facilities without interfering with the competition.

ASSEMBLY AREA

The assembly area is a gathering place for the participants and race officials and also may be where first-aid stations are located. This area should include adequate parking, bicycle racks, changing rooms, and bathrooms. If changing rooms and bathrooms are not available at the site, the participants should be told of this before the race.

A competition often will include having the competitors copy the needed information from the master onto their individual maps before starting out.

It is a good idea to locate the master map area out of sight of the start. A distance of 100 to 150 meters from the start will prevent orienteers from tracking one another.

Shelters can help keep participants and spectators comfortable during inclement or hot weather. These may exist on-site, or you may erect temporary ones. Orienteers gather here to register and receive instructions, maps, control description sheets, control cards, starting times, and numbers or numbered bibs. This is also where competitors study their maps and fill out control cards before moving on to the start.

PACE COURSE

Many beginners may not know their pace, and other competitors may want to check their pace. Set up a pace course over varied terrain for at least 100 meters. A course of 200 to 300 meters is even better. Mark the course with tape and have large signs at 100-meter intervals. Encourage competitors to figure a pace for both walking and running. The pace course is a good place to combine a pace check with warming up.

If there are enough helpers, have one stand at each sign and help young competitors figure out their pace. Even a single helper standing at the beginning of the course can answer enough questions to get first-timers going.

THE START

A recorder and timer's table will be located at the start. After registering, orienteers report to this area and are checked in by the recorder and then released at the proper time by the timer. Intervals between competitors will vary from race to race, depending on the number of participants, the length of the course, and the need to keep the contestants separated.

MASTER MAP AREA

Depending on the rules of the course, competitors will visit the master map area before the competition starts or after each contestant has been released by the timer. If it is before, it is best to have several master maps available (three to five) so that a bottleneck of people waiting to get the information from the map does not develop. If competitors are to visit the map after the start, it is best to space them far enough apart so that only one person will be at the map at a time. Only one or two maps will be needed in this situation.

FINISH

The finish can be at the same place as the start, slightly removed, or in an entirely different place. Different locations usually occur in linear courses rather than in circuit courses. However, just because the course is a circuit does not necessarily mean that contestants will come back to the exact point where they began. It is sometimes better to separate the finish and the start by a short distance to ease congestion and confusion.

When an orienteer reaches the finish, the timer records his finish time on his control card. The timer then passes the card to the recorder, who grades and records the result on the recorder's sheet. The orienteer's standing is determined and posted on the results board.

The orienteer can then take a few minutes to catch his breath, cool down, and get some refreshments. Have at least water available at the site, but juice or sports drinks and fruit, such as oranges and bananas, are welcome. If there is a possibility of inclement weather, it is a good idea to have a place, such as a large tent, where competitors can get out of the rain or wind.

Post approved solution maps for the best routes on the course at the finish. This is a good place for the competitors to compare and discuss how they did with one another. Orienteers can often learn as much from discussing what went right and what went wrong as from actually running the course. More experienced orienteers can be available here to answer questions.

> If the finish is at a different place from the start, you may have to duplicate start facilities there, including parking, bathroom, changing facilities, and a recorder and timer's table.

Course Setting

The course setter or setting team must try to produce a course that will challenge but not discourage the competitors. Do not overestimate the ability of the competitors who will run the course. It is better to make a course too easy than too hard. A competitor may not return to the sport after an initial negative experience. Consider these things:

1. Determine the type of competition. This will help you figure the amount of area needed. Alternatively, design the course to fit the area you have available.

2. Determine the amount of time available for the event. This will give you an idea of the number of control points the course will have.

3. The type of terrain required depends mainly on the experience of the competitors. For most Scouting events, a nearby wooded park is good. Experienced orienteers will find rougher, more complex terrain—even wilderness—desirable.

4. For beginners, the course should not be very complicated. Do not give them too many choices.

5. Avoid dangerous areas such as swift streams, highway crossings, swamps, and utility facilities. When these areas are present, competitors must be well aware of their existence. You can inform competitors by noting these features prominently on the individual maps or by having a briefing before the competition.

6. The course may cross private property only when permission has been obtained from the landowner. To use private property, you may have to provide landowners with liability waivers. Off-limit and private areas should be noted on all maps.

After a bit of preliminary thought and planning, it is time to set off on the actual course-setting. Begin by simply walking the whole area, taking note of the terrain, obstacles, vegetation, prominent land forms, roads, paths, and buildings. When you have a good overview of the area, begin setting the course.

Selecting the Controls

Pick out the "problem" controls (areas that present more of a challenge to the orienteer), for example, whether to go over or around a hill. Plot controls for these key sections on the map. This basic course skeleton along with start and finish locations, the length of the course, and the number of controls will allow you to figure the general shape of the course. It is almost like connecting the dots to get a full picture.

CONTROL DESCRIPTION SHEET

Once you have decided where the controls will be, make a control description sheet for the course. Each contestant will be given one of these sheets at the start of the contest.

Checking the Course

Rarely does the perfect course result from the first attempt. Because so many factors are considered as you set up a course, it is easy to overlook something. It might be best if several Scouts worked on the course together. Afterward, ask your counselors to check the course. This is called *vetting the course*.

Event Officials

At least three officials will be needed at both the start and the finish. They may be the same people for both if the start and finish are at the same location. Their titles and duties are as follows.

At the Start

The **course organizer** briefs orienteers in the assembly area, issues control cards and maps, and calls orienteers forward to start individually. The **recorder** writes the names and start times of every orienteer on the recorder's sheet, checks each orienteer's name and start number on the individual control cards, and issues last-minute instructions. The **timer** controls the master clock and releases the orienteers across the start line at their start time (usually 1 minute apart) to the master map area.

At the Finish

The **timer** records the finish time of each orienteer on his control card and passes the card to the recorder. The **recorder** writes each orienteer's finish times on the recorder's sheet and tallies final scores based on times and correctness of control points visited. The **course organizer** verifies the correctness of names, finish times, and final scores; posts positions of orienteers on the results board; and accounts for all orienteers at the end of the event.

A vetter is an experienced orienteer who checks control placement, routes to the controls, control markers, accuracy of master maps, correctness of descriptive clues, start, finish, and anything else that might affect the result of the competition.

Officiating is the third phase of orienteering besides setting up a course and running in a competition. Each activity will teach you different things about the sport. Participation in all three positions will be rewarding for the knowledge you will gain. There is always room for more officials and assistants, as those listed above are the minimum required to run a competition. *Volunteer!*

Here are a few basic rules for selecting controls:

1. Give careful thought to the actual placing of the control. Beginners will find it easier to locate controls on artificial features. Advanced orienteers will have the skills necessary to identify terrain features as the site of a control.

2. The control must be a definite point, not an area or a linear feature. Orienteering is concerned with precision, not "in the ballpark" direction finding. The fact that an orienteer moves from a definite point at the start and continues to do so throughout the course means his score can be accurately compared with every other competitor's.

3. The control must be a feature that is not only apparent on the ground, but also indicated on the course map. This allows both the course setter and the competitor to locate the control exactly. Avoid vague descriptions such as "an old tree west of the clearing." Courses for inexperienced orienteers should have controls at easy-to-find locations, such as stream junctions, bridges, hilltops, and path junctions.

4. An early leg of the course should not pass near a later control. This will keep competitors from seeing activity near a late control while in the early stages of the race and being able to make use of this knowledge later in their circuit.

5. There should be no sharp angles at the controls. This ensures that the natural exit from a control site is not the same as the entry route, preventing competitors from finding a control by the path of a departing runner. Watch out for unintended doglegs. The map may show no indication of sharp angles from one point to the next, but take a look at the actual ground. Natural features may channel contestants in directions unintended by the course setter, causing competitors to leave a control in full view of oncoming contestants and giving the next competitors an unfair advantage, or at least helping them if they are "lost."

6. The logical route between two controls should not encourage competitors to go over dangerous terrain or cross private property. You can place control points so as to encourage competitors to avoid such areas. The most important rule for course setting is *safety first and always*.

7. In events for experts, the controls should be located so that good orienteers receive due reward. One method of doing this is to place the control on the near side of a collecting feature by several hundred meters. This means that novice orienteers who are off-course will have to retrace their steps from the collecting feature, while good navigators will find the site on their first attempt and will not need the collecting feature.

8. In advanced courses competitors should have to make a route choice on every control. Orienteering allows contestants to travel the route pretty much as they choose, within the constraints of a few rules. This means that orienteers are combining physical skill with navigational skills. A course for beginners can emphasize physical skills because navigation over the ground will still be new. Courses for more advanced orienteers should reward navigation skills as well as physical ability. This can be accomplished by offering subtle route choices between relatively equivalent routes or between good routes and poor ones. The idea is to strive for skill in the decision-making process and not just luck.

9. Select controls so that a variety of problems can be solved on the course. Perhaps the placement of two controls could reward the skill of contouring. Another set might emphasize the use of handrails and attack points. Yet a third might be designed to test compass skills. The course will be more interesting if this is done, and it will teach the competitors more skills as well.

10. Since the spectators, families, and officials see little of the actual competition, it is a good idea to provide a finish where everyone can see a portion of the race. An open run-in of the last 200 meters or so works well. Having the crowd on hand to cheer on the competitors adds a dimension of excitement to the race.

11. Each control marker should be placed where it can be seen easily by someone who has arrived at the feature. Place it head-high and directly over the location given by the clue, visible from 25 meters but not 200 meters away.

Orienteering First Aid

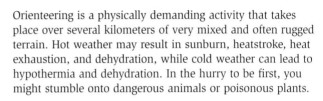

Orienteering is a physically demanding activity that takes place over several kilometers of very mixed and often rugged terrain. Hot weather may result in sunburn, heatstroke, heat exhaustion, and dehydration, while cold weather can lead to hypothermia and dehydration. In the hurry to be first, you might stumble onto dangerous animals or poisonous plants.

Be prepared! Before going out, spend a few minutes reviewing possible injuries and their treatment. Make safety your first priority!

Physical Conditioning

The best thing you can do to prevent injury is to be well-rested, well-fed, and physically fit before going out on an orienteering course. A normal night's sleep and healthy meals will help you endure the rigors of the course and decrease the possibility of a physical or mental slip that could result in injury. Regular exercise such as hiking, running, bicycling, skiing, and snow-shoeing will raise your fitness levels so that any orienteering course is an exhilarating challenge, not a desperate struggle.

Heat-Related Problems

If you are not physically fit, you may be particularly vulnerable to heat.

Dehydration

Dehydration is caused by lack of water in the body. Your body must have water for digestion, respiration, brain activity, and regulation of body temperature. A person who gives off more water than consumed can become dehydrated—in hot *or* cold weather. Athletes can lose up to 14 pounds of fluid in a day. To keep up with this loss, drink 1 to 2 cups of liquid 15 to 20 minutes or so after starting the course and every 15 minutes while on the course. Do not wait to drink until you feel thirsty.

Heat Exhaustion

Heat exhaustion is one result of dehydration. The body becomes overheated because its cooling methods fail. Watch for these signs: elevated body temperature (between 98.6 and 102 degrees); skin pale and clammy—even cool to the touch; heavy sweating; nausea, dizziness, and fainting; pronounced weakness and tiredness; headache; muscle cramps. To treat heat exhaustion, have the victim lie down in a shady, cool spot with the feet raised. Loosen the clothing. Apply cool, damp cloths to the skin or use a fan. Have the victim sip water.

Heatstroke

Heatstroke (sunstroke) is far more serious but less common than heat exhaustion. It is life-threatening because the body's heat control system has been overworked and overwhelmed, resulting in its failure and a skyrocketing body temperature. Watch for these signs: body temperature above 102 degrees (often above 105 degrees); red, hot, and dry skin; no sweating; extremely rapid pulse; confusion or disorientation; fainting or unconsciousness; convulsions. The victim must be cooled immediately. Place the victim in a cool, shaded spot face-up with head and shoulders raised. Remove outer clothing, sponge the bare skin with cold water, and soak underclothing with cool water. Apply cold packs, use a fan, or place the victim in a tub of cold water. Dry the skin after the body temperature drops to 101 degrees. Obtain medical help immediately.

Sunburn

Sunburn is a common but potentially serious result of exposure to sun. Long-term exposure can result in skin damage and skin cancer. The physical effort of orienteering can lure a person into removing clothing to help keep cool, exposing skin to the sun. You can prevent sunburn best by wearing loose-fitting clothing that completely covers the arms and legs and a broad-brimmed hat to shade the neck and face. Apply sunscreen with a sun protection factor (SPF) of at least 15 to exposed skin. Reapply sunscreen often and as needed.

Before heading out, warm up and loosen your muscles by stretching, particularly the thigh and calf muscles and lower-leg tendons.

When applying sunscreen, don't forget your ears and the back of your neck.

Cold-Related Problems—Hypothermia

Hypo means "a lack of"; *thermia* means "heat." Hypothermia occurs when the body's core temperature drops so low that it is no longer possible to keep warm. Hypothermia can happen in relatively mild weather, and the victim may not be aware that there is a problem. Cool, windy, and rainy weather are particularly dangerous. The key to preventing hypothermia is to keep warm and stay dry, and eat plenty of energy foods (nuts, dried fruits, peanut butter). Don't push yourself to a dangerous point of fatigue.

A person in the early stages of hypothermia may be shivering. As the victim becomes even colder, the shivering will stop. Other symptoms may include irritability, disorientation, sleepiness, incoherence, and the inability to think clearly or make rational decisions. In growing confusion, the victim might have no idea that there is any danger and may aggressively reject suggestions to stop and get warm. Rewarm the victim and prevent further heat loss by moving the victim to a shelter, removing damp clothing, and warming the person with blankets until body temperature returns to normal. Cover the head with a warm hat or other covering, and offer hot drinks.

If the condition progresses, you must actively warm the victim's body. Place the victim into a sleeping bag with one or two other people. All should be stripped of clothing so that skin-to-skin contact can hasten the warming—and perhaps save a life. Severe hypothermia requires immediate medical attention.

If you suspect hypothermia because someone is acting strangely, challenge the orienteer to walk a 30-foot line scratched on the ground. If an orienteer can walk heel-to-toe for the length of the line without difficulty, hypothermia is still not a problem. However, unsteadiness, loss of balance, or other signs of disorientation require quick action to see that the orienteer gets warm and dry.

Cuts, Scratches, Puncture Wounds, and Blisters

Running through brush, trees, swampy areas, and uneven terrain on orienteering courses can easily lead to minor injuries. These types of injuries can easily be prevented by dressing appropriately for the activity (jeans, shoes, socks, long sleeves).

Cuts, abrasions, and scratches usually require little attention other than to clean them with soap and water and disinfectant. Leave them to heal in the air, or cover them lightly with a dry, sterile dressing. Unless a cut is serious, bleeding probably will stop on its own or with slight pressure on the wound. Clean and disinfect the wound, then cover with a sterile dressing or bandage.

> Always consider blood to be a potential source of infection; never touch someone else's blood with bare skin. Always use a protective barrier such as disposable gloves, and wash thoroughly afterward with soap and water.

More severe wounds may not stop bleeding readily. Apply direct and firm pressure to such wounds with a sterile dressing or compress. It may help to raise the injured limb (if no bones are broken) above heart-level. Apply pressure to the local artery. If the bleeding is prolonged, treat for shock and seek medical attention immediately.

Puncture wounds, caused by something piercing the skin, often do not bleed very much and are difficult to clean. Encourage bleeding to help remove anything that might have been forced inside the wound. Use sterile tweezers or a sterile needle to pull out any foreign matter that you can see. Clean the wound as thoroughly as possible with soap and water, rinse well with clear water, and apply disinfectant. Allow the wound to air dry, then cover it with a clean, dry bandage.

Tetanus is a very real danger with puncture wounds. Be sure that the injured person sees a physician as soon as possible for a tetanus shot if necessary.

Take precautions to help prevent blisters by using the proper footwear.

Blisters on the feet are common injuries among outdoors enthusiasts, and they can certainly make life miserable. A "hot spot" is a warning that a blister is forming. It is a pinkish area caused by the rubbing of a shoe or boot.

Stop as soon as you notice the discomfort of a hot spot, and treat the area. Cut several pieces of moleskin (every orienteering first-aid kit should have this item) slightly larger than the hot spot. Cut out the center of each piece of moleskin so that it is like a small doughnut, and stack the pieces over the sore area with the holes arranged directly over the most painful part. Tape the stack in place. This will help keep pressure off the hot spot and, with luck, no blister will appear. If a blister does appear, apply a gel pad from the first-aid kit directly over the blister before adding the doughnut bandage. This will help reduce friction and speed healing.

Stings and Bites

Orienteering requires you to be aware of your surroundings and take precautions so that you can stay safe and comfortable. No matter how much insect repellent you apply, stings and bites from insects will happen. The best prevention is to pay attention where you walk, run, and step, and don't place your hands, feet, or head into blind areas of vegetation, wood, or rock. Treat **ordinary insect stings** by scraping the stinger out with the blade of a knife. Don't try to squeeze it out; that will force more venom into the skin. Elevate the affected part, gently wash the area, and apply hydrocortisone cream if you have it.

A wasp, hornet, or bee sting can cause severe allergic reactions in some people. Those people should take a field treatment kit with them on all outings, and their companions should be familiar with its use. If a sting reaction on an arm or leg is particularly severe, isolate its effect by tying a constricting band between the sting and the heart. The band must be loose enough for a finger to slide under it. Cool the wound with water (or ice, if available). Monitor the victim's breathing and do rescue breathing if necessary. Seek medical help.

Fire ant stings can be extremely painful. You can spot fire ants by their distinctive loose mounds of dirt. When disturbed, these aggressive ants will swarm and attack as a group and sting repeatedly. Their stings form tiny blisters; take care not to break the blisters. Wash the injured area well with antiseptic or soap and water, then cover with a sterile bandage.

The **stings of the common scorpion** usually are not as dangerous as bee stings. The stings often cause severe, sharp pain, swelling, and discoloration, but generally cause no lasting ill effects. To relieve itching and pain from a common scorpion sting, apply ice packs or a cold compress if you have it. An over-the-counter antihistamine also can be given. If the victim has a history of allergic reactions to insect stings or shows signs of illness (persistent pain and swelling, numbness, breathing difficulties), and doesn't respond to the prescribed antidote, get medical help as soon as possible.

Rarely, an orienteer may encounter a **venomous spider or scorpion.** Of particular concern are the bites of the black widow spider (identified by a red hourglass on the underside of its abdomen) and the brown recluse spider (recognizable by the fiddle-shaped mark on its back). Less common are stings from the venomous scorpions found in the desert areas of Arizona, California, and New Mexico. A bite or a sting from one of these creatures should be treated in basically the same manner:

- Ice the bite.
- Have the person lie still and, if possible, keep the bite area lower than the heart.
- Tie a constricting band (loose enough to slip a finger between it and the skin) between the bite and the heart.

Bumblebee

If you have 0.5 percent hydrocortisone cream, apply it to help soothe insect stings and bites.

- Treat for shock, and watch for difficulty in breathing; give rescue breathing if required.
- Seek immediate medical attention.

Black widow spider

Brown recluse spider

Always avoid direct contact with a tick because disease can be transmitted by finger contact.

Ticks feed on blood by embedding their head into the skin. They can carry diseases such as Lyme disease and Rocky Mountain spotted fever. Remove a tick as soon as it is discovered by grasping its head as close to the skin as possible with tweezers or gloved fingertips; gently tease the critter from the wound. Don't squeeze, twist, or jerk the tick; that could break off the mouth parts, which would remain in the skin. Wash the wound area carefully with soap and water or an alcohol swab, and apply antiseptic. After handling a tick, wash your hands thoroughly.

Tick

Snakebite

If you are bitten by a snake, assume that it is poisonous unless it can be absolutely identified. The ability to recognize poisonous varieties allows a person to take evasive action when necessary and speeds proper treatment when a bite has occurred.

Two types of poisonous snakes are present in the United States. Pit vipers (rattlesnakes, copperheads, cottonmouths) have triangular-shaped heads with pits on each side in front of the eyes. Coral snakes have black snouts and bands of red and yellow separated by bands of black. Coral snakes inject a powerful venom that works on the nervous system of the victim; pit viper venom affects the circulatory system.

A pit viper bite is likely if there are puncture marks, pain and swelling (possibly severe), skin discoloration, nausea and vomiting, shallow breathing, blurred vision, and shock. A coral snakebite is marked by a slowing of physical and mental reactions, sleepiness, nausea, shortness of breath, convulsions, shock, and coma.

Treatment for either type of poisonous snakebite is best done under medical supervision. Obtain medical help for the victim as quickly as possible. While doing this it is important to limit the spread of the venom and to maintain vital signs. Keep the victim still and the wound below the level of the heart, and tie a broad constricting band an inch or more wide between the bite and the victim's heart (2 to 4 inches above the bite). Do not use constriction bands

Copperhead

Rattlesnake

Cottonmouth moccasin

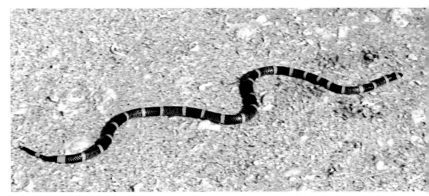

Remember this ditty for safety around coral snakes: red and black—friendly jack; red and yellow–deadly fellow.

on fingers, toes, the head, the neck, or the trunk. Swelling may cause watchbands, rings, clothing, and shoes to restrict circulation. Remove these items in the area of the bite. Treat for shock. Do not apply ice or give alcohol, sedatives, or aspirin.

Poisonous and Pesky Plants

You can prevent most problems with poisonous plants by being able to identify them and by being careful. Poison ivy, poison oak, and poison sumac are the three most common troublemakers; learn how to identify these plants and avoid them.

If you have touched or even just brushed against one of these plants, immediately wash the skin thoroughly with soap and water to help prevent the rash from developing; the sap must be on your skin for 10 to 20 minutes before it causes problems. Further cleanse the area with rubbing alcohol. If a rash develops, apply hydrocortisone cream (0.5 percent strength) if you have it, to help relieve the itching. Scratching the affected area will cause the irritation to spread. Unless the rash becomes severe, further medical attention is not necessary.

Steer clear of the stinging nettle, a wild plant that grows in many parts of the United States. This dreadful plant might attract butterflies, but it stings like a bee. It can grow to more than 6 feet tall. Short spines cover the stem; its leaves are thin and egg-shaped with a tapered tip, and are covered on the underside with short hairs. Its flowers are light green. It is not poisonous (it's actually an herb), but touching the plant releases a very irritating chemical that causes extreme discomfort. If you come into contact with the stinging nettle (also called the bull nettle), do not scratch the affected area. You might get temporary relief by spreading a paste of baking soda mixed with water over the area, or apply vitamin A oil directly to the spot.

Oils from poison ivy, poison oak, and poison sumac can contaminate clothing. Immediately remove and isolate contaminated clothing, and launder as soon as you get home.

Poison oak

Poison ivy

Poison sumac

Orienteering Resources

Scouting Literature

Boy Scout Handbook; *Fieldbook*; *Deck of First Aid*; *Emergency First Aid* pocket guide; *Be Prepared First Aid Book*

Visit the BoyScouts of America's official retal website (with your parent's permission) at http://www.scoutstuff.org for a complete listing of all merit badge pamphlets and other helpful Scouting materials and supplies.

Books

Bagness, Martin. *Outward Bound Orienteering Handbook.* Lyon's Press, 1995.

Boga, Steven. *Orienteering: The Sport of Navigating With Map and Compass.* Stackpole Books, 1997.

Bratt, Ian. *Orienteering: The Essential Guide to Equipment and Techniques.* Stackpole Books, 2002.

Kjellström, Björn. *Be Expert With Map and Compass: The Complete Orienteering Handbook.* Hungry Minds/John Wiley & Sons, 1994.

McNeill, Carol, Tom Renfrew, and Jean Cory-Wright. *Teaching Orienteering, 2nd ed.* Human Kinetics, 1998.

McNeill, Carol. *Orienteering (The Skills of the Game).* Crowood Press, 1996.

Nimvik, Maria, Barbro Rönnberg, and Sue Harvey. *The World of Orienteering.* IOF, 1998.

Norman, Bertil, and Arne Yngström. *Orienteering Technique From Start to Finish.* Sweden, 1991.

Palmer, Peter, ed. *The Complete Orienteering Manual.* Crowood Press, 1998.

Renfrew, Tom. *Orienteering.* Human Kinetics, 1996.

Videocassettes

Braggins and Pearson. *Trail Orienteering,* 21 minutes. A&E Orienteering Inc., 1997

Cassone, Chris. *Orienteering—All Welcome,* 12 minutes. A&E Orienteering Inc., 1998.

Finding Your Way in the Wild: An Easy, Step-by-Step Guide to Using a Map and Compass, 35 minutes. Available from *http://skimaps.altrec.com.*

Orienteering: The First Steps. Part One: Orienteering at School, 25 minutes. Scarborough Orienteering.

Orienteering: The First Steps. Part Two: First Events in the Woods, 25 minutes. Scarborough Orienteering.

Orienteering: Going for It. Part Three: From Light Green to Brown, 27 minutes. Scarborough Orienteering.

Orienteering: Going for It. Part Four: Reaching the Top, 27 minutes. Scarborough Orienteering.

Organizations and Websites

Canadian Orienteering Federation
Website: http://www.orienteering.ca

International Orienteering Federation
Website: http://www.orienteering.org

U.S. Geological Survey
12201 Sunrise Valley Drive
Reston, VA 20192
Telephone: 703-648-4000
Website: http://www.usgs.gov

Orienteering USA
P.O. Box 1444
Forest Park, GA 30298-1444
Website: http://www.orienteeringusa.org

Equipment Sources

A&E Orienteering
P.O. Box 443
Baldwin City, KS 66006
Telephone: 785-594-3516
Website: http://www.aeorienteering.com

Berman's Orienteering Supply
23 Fayette St.
Cambridge, MA 02139
Telephone: 617-868-7416

The Compass Store
ROC Gear
5210 Palmero Ct., Suite 104
Buford, GA 30518
Telephone: 678-318-3660
Website:
http://www.thecompassstore.com

Orienteering Unlimited Inc.
3 Jan Ridge Road
Somers, NY 10589-3007
Telephone: 914-248-5957
Website:
http://www.orienteeringunlimited.com

Scarborough Orienteering
3015 Holyrood Drive
Oakland, CA 94611
Telephone: 510-530-3059
Website: http://orienteer.com

U.S. Geological Survey Topographic Maps

A local sporting goods store or bookstore may carry topographic maps of your area. You can also find local dealers in your state at the U.S. Geological Survey website, http://www.usgs.gov.
Or send a postcard to the National Cartographic Information Center, 507 National Center, 12201 Sunrise Valley Drive, Reston, VA 20192.

Ask for a free topographic map index circular of your state. The index circular is a small map of the state divided into sections called quadrangles. Each quadrangle is a separate map. Find out which quadrangles cover the area in which you want to orienteer. Order the map by giving the name of the quadrangle and include a money order or check for payment. Send your order to Branch Distribution, U.S. Geological Survey, Box 25286, Federal Center, Denver, CO 80225.

Acknowledgments

The Boy Scouts of America is grateful to Eagle Scout and longtime Scouter Ralph Courtney and to Miki Snell, Peter Snell, Tatyana Svistun, and Sergey Svistun for their time, patience, and technical knowledge in support of this new edition of the *Orienteering* merit badge pamphlet. Special thanks to Ralph Courtney and to Tatyana Svistun and Sergey Svistun for their assistance with many of the maps depicted in this pamphlet.

The General Rules for Orienteering are adapted with permission from *Orienteering: The Sport of Navigating With Map and Compass,* by Steven Boga, Stackpole Books, 1997. The early history of orienteering is adapted with permission from *Orienteering: The Sport of Navigating With Map and Compass,* by Steven Boga, Stackpole Books, 1977, and from *The Complete Orienteering Manual,* by Peter Palmer, ed., The Crowood Press, 1998.

Thanks to the International Orienteering Federation for its assistance with the international control description symbols.

Illustrations are adapted with permission from *Be Expert With Map and Compass,* by Bjorn Kjellstrom, Hungry Minds, 1994, and *Mountaineering: The Freedom of the Hills,* 5th ed., by Don Graydon, ed., The Mountaineers, 1992.

The Sid Richardson Scout Ranch (East) SR2 orienteering map is reprinted with permission of the Longhorn Council, Fort Worth, Texas.

Photo and Illustration Credits

Lisa Ames, University of Georgia, *Bugwood.org,* courtesy—page 70 *(top left)*

Ronald F. Billings, Texas Forest Service, *Bugwood.org,* courtesy—page 70 *(top right)*

Longhorn Council, Boy Scouts of America, courtesy—Sid Richardson Scout Ranch orienteering map used on the cover, in photographs, and on pages 10, 29, 31, 38, 40–42, and 47

©Photos.com—page 69

USDA Agricultural Resource Service/ Scott Bauer, *Bugwood.org,* courtesy— page 70 *(bottom)*

U.S. Fish and Wildlife Service/Luther C. Goldman, courtesy—page 72

Wikipedia.org, courtesy— page 71 *(center)*

Wikipedia.org/John Wilson, Savannah River Ecology Laboratory, courtesy— page 71 *(bottom)*

Wikipedia.org/Edward J. Wozniak, DVM, Ph.D., courtesy—page 71 *(top)*

All other photos and illustrations not listed above are the property of or are protected by the Boy Scouts of America.

John McDearmon—cover *(taking a bearing illustrations);* pages 8 *(illustration),* 9, 12 *(all),* 54, and 68

Dan Bryant—pages 5–6 *(both)*

Darrell Byers—pages 7 and 25

Brian Payne—pages 24, 44, 46, and 48

Randy Piland—pages 25 and 73 *(poison ivy)*

Notes

Notes

Notes

Notes